EAT DESSERT FIRST

Written, collected and edited by
STEPHEN WILSON
Psychologist and THE JOYOLOGIST

Illustrations by
SENETT

APPLIED HUMOR SYSTEMS

Printed on re-cycled paper.

"The Wizards of AHS"

ISBN: 089894-048-6

COVER DESIGN: SENETT
ART: SENETT
CARTOONS: SENETT

10 9 8 7 6 5 4 3 2 1

Printed in the United States

Advocate Publishing Group

1292 - 8A Stonecreek Drive N.W.
Pickerington, Ohio 43147

Life is uncertain . . . eat dessert first!

Who Said That???

Indexing

NOTE 1: Author's names do not appear with each quotation or idea. This is done purposely to allow you to be as open-minded as possible about the truth of each statement. You can consider each statement "on its own," without regard to race, gender, age, politics, etc., of the author. As Al Schneider puts it, "All persons are but conduits through which all ideas pass from the original creative reservoir."

NOTE 2: At the back of the book is a complete indexing of statements by author which is cross-indexed by quotation number. You can determine the author of any statement, and you can find all statements attributed to each author. It is impossible to ascertain the source of every statement, and I apologize to those who should have received name credit.

Table of Contents

Dedication

For the universal extended family of laughers everywhere, especially the ones who laugh out loud at cartoons, comic strips, and the written word; especially my personal favorite, Pam.

Very Special Thanks

To my mother, Shirley Kalter Wilson, who, in her teens was a Flapper; she taught me that love and laughter and playfulness are strengths;

To my father, Jack Wilson, who laughs to the point of tears and teaches me to appreciate humor, intelligence, dignity, and perserverance;

To my step-mom Helen Wilson, who has a highly contagious laugh and gives consistent encouragement;

To my sister, Phyllis, who, thank God, finds the humor in any and every situation;

To my kids: Shawn, Jenifer, Rachel, Josh, and Bethany who put up with my jokes, and inspire me to hard work by their incessant demands for food, clothing, and shelter, and now they want to go to college, too!;

And, mostly, to my wife, Pam, stalwart booster, companion, lover, fantastic homemaker, excellent cook, shrewd business manager, caring mother, loving daughter, for so many wonderful one-day-at-a-times and (. . . was there anything else you told me to say, dear?).

Acknowledgements

The EAT DESSERT FIRST project has brought me extreme pleasure. It is in every respect a labor of love. It is my way of giving the world a gift which is partial repayment on my cosmic debt for blessings too numerous to recount here.

Many people, whether or not they are aware of it, have contributed to the success of my work as a JOYOLOGIST and helped make this book possible.

Thanks from the bottom of my heart to everyone who ever believed in me over the years, especially when I was most unbelievable. To my family and friends, co-workers, colleagues and students, clients, and the tens of thousand of people who have attended my lectures, seminars and PLAYSHOP LABS.

Thanks to Joel Goodman who showed me not only that Laughing Matters, but what the possibilities are; to every presenter and participant at the I.A.H.B. and Humor Project conferences; to Jim Pelley, The Wunderkind, about whom I, myself, kinda' wunder sometimes, but who is determined to prove that Laughter Works!

Thanks to the dear and generous people who let me do my thing for their employees and organizations; to the patients, nurses, and physicians in numerous health care facilities who shared their experiences with me.

Thanks to author Robert Shook who looked at the first draft of this book and told me not to give up my day job; to Terry Wike whose great confidence is ever a source of encouragement, not to mention all the stamps he licked for the CAUSE; to Rae Murphy who always knew I could do it.

Thanks to all of my Humor Penpals across North America who fill my days with hope and energy which is the natural consequence of caring relationships that share humor and good fun.

Thanks to all of the teachers, entertainers, artists, and writers who made me laugh and taught me an appreciation for many *different* senses of humor.

Thanks to my faithful partners, Michael Senett and Steve White, the Wizards of AHS.

And, not because of any lack of appreciation, but due to the limitations of memory, thanks to everyone I did not put into this list but who was just as meaningful. In a sense, you taught me everything I know.
Again, thank you.

S. W.

My Philosophy

This book is dedicated to the proposition
that life, no matter how long, is too short;
laughter too scarce; playtime ends too
soon. "Now" is the most important time;
Too much seriousness is hazardous to your
health;
Silliness cures many maladies;
Smile lines look better than worry lines;
Joy destroys stress;
All living things long to love and be loved;
Humor creates and sustains an atmosphere
of love, support, and understanding;
We all need more fun;
Foolishness can be the wisest way;
and, everybody—*absolutely everybody*—
can locate and strengthen their sense of
humor!

STEPHEN WILSON
THE JOYOLOGIST

The creator made man able to do everything—talk, run, look and hear. He was not satisfied, though, till man could do just one thing more—and that was: LAUGH. And so man laughed and laughed. And the creator said,

"Now you are fit to live."

—Apache Indian myth

Introduction: The Power of Your Laughter

The Promise

Walt Disney—and Uncle Remus' Brer Rabbit—pointed out that "everyone has a laughing place" that can get us through and out of a lot of troubles. "Some people" he said, "just don't take time to find it." I hope you will make this book one of your laughing places and I encourage you to take the time to find other laughing places for yourself.

For one thing, this book is just for fun, and you don't need any particular reason to read it. And, for those who feel the need, it is a source from which to develop your sense of humor and reap the benefits of the laughter and pleasure which naturally follow.

Around the globe there is an awakening. Some say we are in a "New Age" (although the *truth* is really "age old"): we must learn to appreciate our world from its awesome majesty to its tiniest details, or we will lose it. The promise to us, if we will respect and care for our planet and all living things, is clarity of vision, peace, and joy.

"Joy is the most infallible sign of the presence of God."

—Teilhard de Chardin

"Even the Gods love jokes."

—Plato

"A man hath no better thing under the sun than to eat and to drink and to be merry."

—Ecclesiastes

"The halls of heaven ring with laughter of the saints."

—Master Hilarion

"When you finally allow yourself to trust joy and embrace it, you will find you dance with everything."

—Emmanuel

"The world will end in joy . . The world will end in peace The world will end in laughter."

—A Course in Miracles

And here is an interesting twist. To receive this promise, many of us will have to "unlearn" rather than learn; give up our conservative, conventional thinking about what is "safe" and do things differently, which will include developing the habit of enjoying guilt-free pleasure. Annette Goodheart, Ph.D., a psychotherapist specializing in *laughter* therapy, says, "If your aim is to be a thinking, caring, communicative person, you need to take the risk and laugh."

Give yourself permission to be a little less practical and a lot more comfortable. Change some of your habitual ways of doing things; get out of your rut. "Make the most of each day" is not a new idea but one that most people appreciate being reminded of from time to time.

The Present

Many people plan and save for—and dream of—a distant future they may never live to see. The truth is, if you make a practice of finding pleasures in the present moments, your life will fill with richness and happiness. The time to begin the practice of enjoying each moment is now.

"If I fill up on vegetables and meat and potatoes," and old-timer once told me,"I may not have room for a delicious dessert. So, once in a while, I eat dessert first to be sure I don't miss out on it."

"Life Is Uncertain:" a bumper sticker warns, "Eat Dessert First". Another suggests we "Enjoy life: this is not a dress rehearsal," and another recommends "Don't Postpone Joy!" It seems to me that these philosophical nuggets arise out of the sort of surprise personal experiences which serve as lessons for you and me that the future is not guaranteed to anyone.

On a daily basis, the airwaves waft the musical exhortation, "Don't Worry, Be Happy". And this kind of wisdom has even been received in a fortune cookie: "We live in an eternity; the time to be happy is now."

There is now a crescendo of realization that although you can live for tomorrow, tomorrow may not come. Read the obituaries and you will see that a lot of folks did not get up this morming; you did, and this is the day—and the *only day*—you are given in which to be happy. Today is the day to enjoy yourself.

This is not a call for wanton hedonism. It is a thoughtful recognition of the fantastic, marvelous condition we call "life," and a respect for its delicate balance, our limited life-span, and the potential for enjoyment. At times it comes across to me as a happy spirituality.

The Power

Apply it properly and *EAT DESSERT FIRST!* can become a remedy for overcoming any limitations of your ability to experience unbridled pleasure and fun in life. I encourage you to use it just for fun and as a tonic for those times when you are besieged with setbacks whether they are physical, mental, emotional, occupational, relational, financial, or spiritual.

For thousands of years educators, philosophers, humorists, poets, spiritual leaders, scientists, royalty, and common folk around the world have observed and reported on the seeming powers of humor, laughter, and playfulness. *EAT DESSERT FIRST!* is a collection of hundreds of those observations and ideas, to which scientists are now adding increasing evidence that the *amazing* power of your laughter is the natural endowment of human beings.

The Positive

At this point, let's be clear that not all humor is helpful and not all laughter indicates pleasure. There is a great deal of negative humor which is caustic, barbed, sarcastic, demeaning, and meant to humiliate. Negative humor destroys; it emphasizes our differences in a derogatory way. It is dishonest and bigoted: sexist, racist, ageist, and angry. You may see people laughing on the outside while inside they are in agony. Positive humor is loving, kind, truthful, inclusive, and builds people, up; it celebrates each one's uniqueness. It heals.

This book is about promoting enjoyment of living through positive humor.

With laughter, positive humor, and an element of playfulness we are less stressed, healthier, more attractive, more resistant to illness, more creative, productive, happier, and more satisfied.

With positive humor we learn more quickly, retain information longer, relax more readily, heal faster, defuse anger and anxiety, are more persuasive, recruit more customers, sell more products, win friends, entertain ourselves, cope with oppression, chase away depression, and fight against repression.

With positive humor we can see TRUTH more clearly which means we are more likely to see the world as the universal force of creation meant for us to see it: awesome, wonderful, pleasure-filled, joyful.

Of course, not everything in life is laughable. There are tragedies and there is a time to cry. Yet, consider this: the average pre-school child in the U.S.A. laughs 400 times a day, but the average adult in this country laughs only about 15 times a day. This means that between childhood and adulthood we lose 385 laughs a day. We can't afford the loss! This book is a way of recapturing some of the lost laughs all human beings need so much.

Did you know that you don't have to teach anybody how to laugh or smile? Human beings have those abilities virtually from birth. However, while smiling and laughing are inborn human abilities, the *sense* of humor must be developed, and it simply does not come easily to many people. Even when we are able to remember jokes, ninety-five percent of us cannot tell them very well; nor can we think of snappy comebacks for zingers when someone hits us with them until two hours—or two days—later when it's, "I know what I should have said to him!!!"

If this sounds like you, don't give up, because, in addition to telling jokes, there are hundreds of ways that you can bring warmth, smiles, humor, and laughter to yourself and others. For example, reading, re-reading, and *using* this book are some very good ways.

When you or someone you know loses touch with that *sense* of humor, or when the world isn't giving you much reason to laugh, don't despair. You can use this book to help recover your balance. Or, if you have a sense of humor and want to enhance it, or if you just need a lift, this book will become a traveling companion on your journey to brighter spirits.

In EAT DESSERT FIRST you will find more than 400 wise and witty observations about humor, reminding you and giving you permission to experience more of the pleasures and joys of living. Through the dozens of Michael Senett's fabulous cartoons and drawings you will find the most delightful and hilarious visual expression of these uplifting and thought-provoking ideas.

Many, many funny things happened on the way to putting this book together. We tried out dozens of creative ideas as we generated and refined the concept. We laughed, adapted and adopted some of the ideas, laughed, decided to save some ideas for future volumes, laughed, felt exhilarated, laughed, felt inspired, and laughed and laughed and laughed! And laughing *a lot* is exactly what we hope you will do, too.

It is my sincere wish that *EAT DESSERT FIRST* will help you live each day more fully, love yourself and others more completely, laugh more often, and be more playful, healthy, and happy.

Steve Wilson, Psychologist

-1-

Don't Postpone Joy!

-2-

To laugh often and much, to win the respect of intelligent people and the affection of children . . . to leave the world a bit better . . . to know even one life had breathed easier because you have lived, that is to have succeeded.

∮

-3-

There are many different "senses" of humor. It's different jokes for different folks.

∮

-4-

Genuine humor is always kindly and gracious. It points out the weakness of humanity, but shows no contempt and leaves no sting.

∮

-5-

If you can't remember a joke—don't dismember it.

-6-

"Over the years, I have encountered a surprising number of instances in which, to all appearances, patients have laughed themselves back to health, or at least have used their sense of humor as a very positive and adaptive response to their illness."

-7-

It's no coincidence that the man I know who always has the best stock of new jokes is not a comedian, but a salesman.

∳

-8-

It is great to be great, but it's greater to be human.

∳

FUNNY BONES

Whoever named it necking was a poor judge of anatomy.

—Groucho Marx

-9-

Humorous advertising is doing the job. The consumer has so many distractions, so much to do, so much information clamoring for his attention, that off-beat advertising is about the only decent way of getting and holding his attention.

-10-

Humor is tragedy plus time.

∮

-11-

One of the best things people can have up their sleeves is a funnybone.

∮

-12-

Things are getting so bad, according to one authority, the meek no longer want to inherit the earth.

∮

-13-

A closed mouth gathers no feet.

-14-

Computers will never replace man entirely
until they learn to laugh at the boss's jokes.

-15-

Humorists always sit at the children's table.

∮

-16-

Laughter and good humor are the canaries in the mine of commerce. If you and your employees, customers, and vendors don't have a good time, if the laughter has died, you're in the wrong business.

∮

-17-

He who hesitates is not only lost but several miles from the next exit.

∮

-18-

You can turn painful situations through laughter. If you can find humor in anything—even poverty—you can survive it.

-19-

Serious writings on laughter are often so absurd as to be laughable.

∮

-20-

A smile is a curve that sets
everything straight.

∮

-21-

In spite of the cost of living,
it's still popular.

∮

-22-

My way of joking is to tell the truth. It's
the funniest joke in the world.

∮

-23-

Long ago I used to think that the
cartoonists—the comic strip artists—who
make us laugh with our morning coffee are
about the most important people in the
world. Now . . . more than ever, these
people deserve our gratitude.

FUNNY BONES

A woman in love will do almost anything for a man, except give up the desire to improve him.

—Nathanial Branden

∮

-24-

The pursuit of happiness seems to be the chase of a lifetime.

∮

-25-

The wit thinks while he's talking, or, even worse, while you're talking.

∮

-26-

We are all here for a spell. Get all the good laughs you can.

-27-

The trouble with the rat race is that even if you win, you're still a rat.

-28-

When a thing is funny, look for a hidden truth.

∮

-29-

Humor and boredom are incompatible; humor changes ho-hum into ho-ho, and run-of-the-mill changes into fun-of-the-mill.

∮

-30-

You can discover more about a person in an hour of play than in a year of conversation.

∮

FUNNY BONES

The most difficult years of marriage are those following the wedding.

—Unknown

-31-

The really happy person is the one who can enjoy the scenery on a detour.

-32-

The most wasted day of all is that on which we have not laughed.

∮

-33-

Imagination was given to us to compensate for what we are not; a sense of humor was provided to console us for what we are.

∮

-34-

Happiness is not having what you want, it's wanting what you have.

∮

-35-

The fellow who can smile when things go wrong is probably just going off shift.

-36-

A clown is like an aspirin, only he works twice as fast.

-37-

Humor is falling downstairs if you do it while in the act of warning your wife not to.

∮

-38-

You grow up the day you have your first real laugh—at yourself.

∮

-39-

A sense of humor divides troubles, subtracts stresses, and multiplies opportunities; adds up, doesn't it?

∮

-40-

Perhaps I know best why it is man alone who laughs; he alone suffers so deeply that he had to invent laughter.

-41-

As a family practitioner, I see not only what kind of disease each patient has, but what kind of *patient* each *disease* has.

∮

-42-

When someone blushes with embarassment . . . , when someone carries away an ache . . . , when something sacred is made to appear common . . . , when someone's weakness provides the laughter . . . , when profanity is required to make it funny . . . , when a child is brought to tears . . . or when everyone can't join in the laughter . . . , it's a poor joke!

∮

-43-

Some pursue happiness—others create it.

∮

FUNNY BONES

I don't see much of Alfred anymore since he got interested in sex.

—Mrs. Alfred Kinsey

-44-

Patience is something you admire greatly in the driver behind you but not in the one ahead of you.

∮

-45-

Wrinkles should merely indicate where the smiles have been.

∮

-46-

If I can get you to laugh with me, you like me better, which makes you more open to my ideas.

∮

-47-

Humor affirms our humanity.

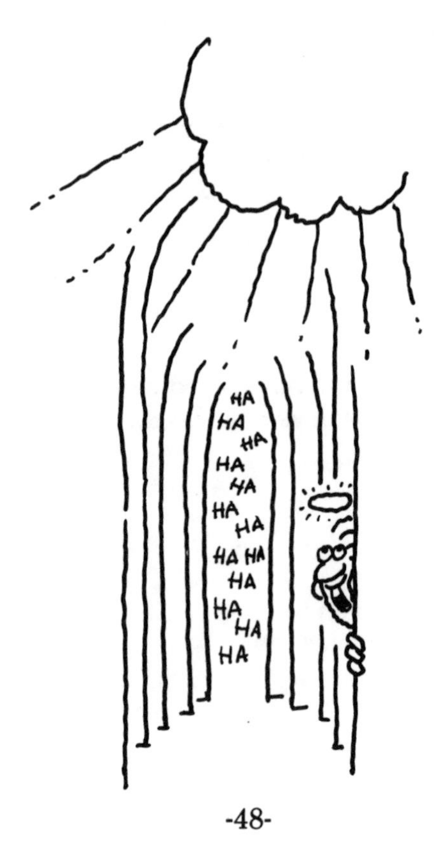

-48-

The halls of heaven ring with the laughter of the saints.

-49-

The saying, "Don't worry" can be improved immeasurably if you add the word "others."

∮

-50-

There is a hell of a distance between wisecracking and wit. Wit has truth in it; wisecracking is simply calisthenics with words.

∮

-51-

Every man is a damn fool for at least five minutes every day; wisdom consists of not exceeding the limit.

∮

FUNNY BONES

Sex appeal is 50% what you've got and 50% what people think you've got.

—Sophia Loren

-52-

Don't get discouraged. No one is perfeck.

∮

-53-

Humor is really laughing off a hurt, grinning at misery.

∮

-54-

Humor appeals to a sense of enjoyment rather than a sense of logic. Know the numbers and have the product information, but your sales efforts should approach an individual's mind, emotions, and funny bone. You can't reason with people who aren't paying attention.

∮

-55-

If you watch a game, it's fun. If you play it, it's recreation. If you work at it, it's golf.

-56-

A playful attitude is best.

∮

-57-

Television is a medium. They call it that because a lot of the stuff you see on it is neither rare nor well done.

∮

FUNNY BONES

Giving a man space is like giving a dog a computer: The chances are he will not use it wisely.

—Bette-Jane Raphael

∮

-58-

Laughter is not at all a bad beginning for a friendship, and it is far the best ending for one.

-59-

If you would rule the world quietly, you must keep it amused.

-60-

One of the greatest mysteries of life is how the idiot that your daughter married can be the father of the smartest grandchildren in the whole wide world.

∮

-61-

Your ulcers can't grow while you're laughing.

∮

-62-

The power of humor is enormous.

∮

-63-

Humor is part of our strategy.

-64-

A mime is a terrible thing to waste.

-65-

There is no medicine like hope, no incentive so great, and no tonics so powerful as expectation of something better tomorrow.

∮

-66-

The way to maximize your creativity is to cultivate as much inner joy as possible and give yourself all the permission you need to enjoy yourself fully.

∮

-67-

When you play the fool, you play from strength.

∮

-68-

Happiness is like a butterfly. The more you chase it, the more it will elude you. But if you turn your attention to other things, it comes and softly sits on your shoulder.

-69-

Without laughter, the spiritual path would be boring.

∮

-70-

It is when humor restores proportion that our blind eye is open.

∮

FUNNY BONE

The closest to perfection a person ever comes is when s/he fills out a job application form.

—Stanley J. Randall

∮

-71-

The effects of pleasure are wholly positive.

-72-

Though a humorist may bomb occasionally, it is still better to exchange humorists than bombs. And . . . you can't fight when you're laughing.

∮

-73-

Let the surgeon take care to regulate the whole regimen of the patient's life for joy and happiness.

∮

-74-

An optimist goes to the window every morning and says, "Good morning, Lord." The pessimist goes to the window and says, "Good Lord, morning!"

∮

-75-

The salesman's customer is his audience. He must "make friends" much in the same way the comedian establishes a rapport with his listeners.

-76-

God is not totally serious, and therefore neither do I have to be.

∮

-77-

A sense of humor is what makes you laugh at something that would make you mad if it happened to you.

∮

FUNNY BONES

Give a man a free hand and he'll run it over you.

—Mae West

-78-

If you can laugh at it, you can live with it.

∮

-79-

There are very few good judges of humor, and they don't agree.

-80-

If you want to learn (how to have fun), spend some time with a child who knows how to have a good time.

-81-

Laughter is to life what salt is to an egg.

∮

-82-

If you cannot see the lighter side of an issue, you can be certain that you have lost your way. And when you can laugh about it, you have found your way.

∮

-83-

Happiness consists of living each day as if it were the first day of your honeymoon and the last day of your vacation.

∮

-84-

A man isn't really poor if he can still laugh.

-85-

"Education doesn't have to be fun,
but it helps."

§

FUNNY BONES

A committee is twelve people doing the work of one.

—J. F. Kennedy

§

-86-

"Freddie, you musn't laugh out loud in the schoolroom." "I didn't mean to do it. I was smiling, and the smile busted."

§

-87-

Laughter is one of the most important aids to digestion . . . the nourishment received amid mirth and jollity is productive of light and healthy blood . . ."

-88-

Nurse's Song

When the voices of children are heard on
the green
And laughing is heard on the hill,
My heart is at rest within my breast
And everything else is still.

"Then come home, my children, the sun is
gone down
And the dews of night arise;
Come, come, leave off play, and let us away
Till morning appears in the skies.

"No, no, let us play, for it is yet day
And we cannot go to sleep;
Besides, in the sky the little birds fly
And the hills are cover'd with sheep.

"Well, well, go & play till the light fades
away
And then go home to bed."
And the little ones leaped & shouted and
Laugh'd
And all the hills echoed.

-89-

Humor can be found in Zen, in the Native American cultures, in the Jewish and Hindu traditions . . . and in many others. In all of them, masters, holy fools, and sages are cherished as inexhaustible sources of sanity, healing, and wholeness. Their laughter, in the words of Yuan-Wo, is "like a cool, refreshing breeze passing through the source of all things."

-90-

Life is a tragedy when seen in close-up, but a comedy in longshot.

∮

-91-

The more confident you are, the less afraid you will be of looking stupid. You may need to learn how to relax and do nothing.

∮

-92-

There are no language barriers when you are smiling.

∮

-93-

Laughter removes the burden of seriousness from the problem and oftentimes, it's that very serious attitude that is the problem itself.

-94-

If the animals suddenly got the gift of laughter, they'd start by laughing themselves sick about man.

-95-

The trouble with mixing business and pleasure is that pleasure usually comes out on top.

∮

-96-

The person who loses his head is usually the last to miss it.

∮

FUNNY BONES

Don't assume that every sad-eyed woman has loved and lost—she may have got him.

—Unknown

∮

-97-

The human need to play is a powerful one. When we ignore it we feel there is something missing in our lives.

-98-

A real friend is a person who, when you've made a fool of yourself, lets you forget it.

∮

-99-

You are much happier when you are happy than when you ain't.

∮

-100-

Humor can be dissected as a frog can, but the thing dies in the process and the innards are discouraging to any but the pure scientist.

∮

-101-

Do not take life too seriously; you will never get out of it alive.

-102-

Laughter is the musical accompaniment to life composed by Mother Nature.

-103-

Our "child" lies dormant within each of us and our normal, intended state is to be healthy, magical, and childlike.

∮

-104-

Despair affects the immune system . . . I try to leave patients with something to smile about.

∮

-105-

Life does not cease to be funny when people die any more than it ceases to be serious when people laugh.

∮

-106-

People do not stop playing because they grow old. They grow old because they stop playing.

-107-

A toast: May all your pleasures become habits.

∮

-108-

Natural childlike qualities are the true essences of life. They are the magic we should seek to recapture.

∮

-109-

One of the things I learned the hard way was that it doesn't pay to get discouraged. Keeping busy and making optimism a way of life can restore your faith in yourself.

∮

-110-

Lessen your tension and enjoy your pension.

-111-

If we have to leave the stage, we might as well dance off in a chorus of chuckles instead of a dirge of doom.

-112-

There are two things that everyone must face sooner or later: a camera and reality. A smile is a big help in both instances.

∮

-113-

If you can laugh at it, you can do battle with it.

∮

-114-

Humor is the high road into and through transformation.

∮

-115-

Don't let dogged determination kill your sense of fun. An element of playfulness will make you more creative, more satisfied and, yes, more productive, too.

-116-

Enjoy Yourself, It's Later Than You Think.

∮

FUNNY BONES

For a while, we pondered whether to take a vacation or get a divorce. We decided that a trip to Bermuda is over in two weeks, but a divorce is something you always have.

—Woody Allen

∮

-117-

Find pleasure in little things: food that tastes delicious, friendship that is sincere, a sun that is warming, a smile meant to cheer.

∮

-118-

Laughter is the only form of revolution we have left in this country.

-119-

Everything is funny as long as it is happening to someone else.

-120-

You don't have to teach people to be funny.
You only have to give them permission.

∮

-121-

Laughter is free, legal, has no calories, no cholesterol, no preservatives, no artificial ingredients, absolutely safe.

∮

-122-

Against the assault of humor, nothing can stand.

∮

-123-

A good mental attitude can influence the body's healing mechanism.

-124-

Humor results when society says you can't scratch certain things in public, but they itch in public.

-125-

Men will confess to treason, arson, false teeth or a wig. How many of them will own up to a lack of a sense of humor?

∮

-126-

People are funnier than anybody.

∮

-127-

You never outgrow your need for JOY!

∮

-128-

People who are able to laugh and have a positive outlook heal in half the time as do people with the same illness receiving the same treatment.

∮

-129-

Some things have to be believed to be seen.

-130-

Learn to laugh, especially at yourself. Learn to have fun and be a little silly and crazy. In other words, "lighten up." When you do this, the whole world will seem brighter and more beautiful.

-131-

Imagination is more important than knowledge.

∮

-132-

A sense of humor reduces people and their problems to their proper proportions.

∮

FUNNY BONES

Some husbands are living proof that a woman can take a joke.

—Unknown

∮

-133-

In the end, everything is a gag.

-134-

A sense of humor will help take the bite out of whatever's eating you.

∲

-135-

In Native American circles humor is commonly used as a corrective or a way of deflecting hostility into a lesson.

∲

-136-

Laughter is the shortest distance between two people.

∲

-137-

A smiling face has more appeal—perhaps even more sex appeal—than a nonsmiling one.

-138-

Wherever you go in "Indian Country" you will find laughter—a laughter which may be bawdy one minute, sacred the next. But whichever it is, you can be sure that it is a humor which makes its points clearly to Native Americans, and those points include the importance of humility and the affirmation that laughter leads to learning and survival.

-139-

The greatest prayer you could ever pray would be to laugh everyday.

∮

-140-

Laugh intentionally, live un-tension-ally.

∮

-141-

A true sense of humor is shown in the ability to laugh at one's self.

∮

-142-

Humor is the lubricating oil of business. It prevents friction and wins good will.

-143-

When humor is present we lose not seriousness, but only solemnity.

∮

-144-

Good humor is goodness and wisdom combined.

∮

-145-

Indeed, the Indians did joke, and the forest more often rang with their laughter than it did with their war whoops.

∮

-146-

Laughter is too good a thing to be left to chance.

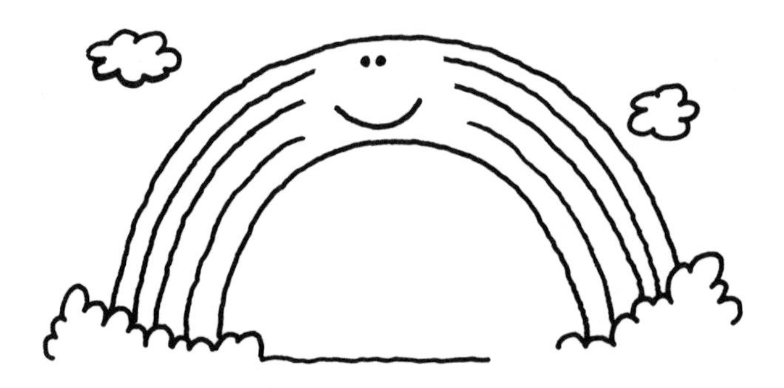

-147-

Joy is the most infallible sign of the presence of God.

-148-

An optimist laughs to forget; a pessimist forgets to laugh.

∮

-149-

Fortune smiles upon the man who can laugh at himself.

∮

FUNNY BONES

Men are more interesting than women, but women are more fascinating.

—James Thurber—

∮

-150-

If you understand what makes a people laugh, you are closer to understanding and appreciating them.

-151-

Laughter is the natural sound of childhood.

∮

-152-

People who feel good about themselves
produce good results.

∮

-153-

I don't make jokes. I just watch the
government and report the facts.

∮

-154-

Enjoy life. This is not a dress rehearsal!

-155-

It's remarkable how many bright people work for dumb bosses.

§

-156-

When my children were very young, during summer vacation in the country they used to disappear after dinner with the neighbor's children. Sometimes the only way we knew where they were was to listen for their laughter.

§

-157-

What sunshine is to flowers, smiles are to humanity.

§

FUNNY BONES

Never go to bed mad. Stay up and fight.

—Phyllis Diller

-158-

Nothing improves a joke more than telling it to your employees.

-159

Going bananas once in a while sure can help a bunch.

∮

-160-

The value of being able to laugh at ourselves when we make a mistake: it helps us get on with our work.

∮

-161-

Life without joy and song and playfulness is incomplete.

∮

-162-

Necessity may be the mother of invention, but play is certainly the father.

-163-

If you're too busy to laugh, you're entirely too busy.

-164-

Jewish humor . . . has in some ways come to replace the standard sacred texts as a touchstone for the entire Jewish community. Not all Jews can read and understand a page of the Talmud, but even the most assimilated tend to have a special affection for Jewish jokes.

∮

-165-

To travel hopefully is a better thing than to arrive.

∮

-166-

Joys shared are doubled, sorrows shared are halved.

∮

-167-

A well-balanced person is one who finds both sides of an issue laughable.

-168-

America is a country where Groucho Marx
has more followers than Karl Marx.

-169-

The real magic in life is not a trick.

∮

-170-

The person who laughs at the boss's jokes doesn't necessarily have a sense of humor, but s/he surely has a sense of direction.

∮

-171-

It is paradoxical that many educators and parents still differentiate between a time for learning and a time for play without seeing the vital connection between them.

∮

-172-

Jokes of the proper kind, properly told, can do more to enlighten questions of politics, philosophy, and literature than any number of dull arguments.

-173-

Of course, it's very easy to be witty tomorrow, after you get a chance to do some research and rehearse your ad libs.

∮

-174-

One good hearty laugh together could be the greatest insurance of lasting peace that people of all nations could contrive.

∮

-175-

The great man is he who does not lose his child's heart.

∮

-176-

We become devoid of humor when we are pompous, pretentious, obviously hiding an unmistakable feeling of inferiority.

-177-

People show their character in nothing more clearly than what they think laughable.

-178-

The things you worry about most
never happen.

∮

-179-

The more you share your happiness with
others, the more you have yourself.

∮

-180-

I would rather be with someone who is
"acting" cheerful than someone who is
sincerely grouchy.

∮

-181-

Humor is good for your health and that of
your employees. Healthy, happy employees
are on the job. Unhappy ones tend to call in
"sick"—and they may well be.

-182-

Being fun to do business with usually results in doing a lot more business.

-183-

People rarely succeed at anything unless they have fun doing it.

∮

-184-

When you are happy, the glorious things in nature are more visible, the flowers smell better, the sound of a rippling brook is more distinct, food tastes better, the hand of friendship is firmer, and your voice has more life to it.

∮

-185-

Humor is a fine teaching tool. People learn when they are enjoying themselves.

∮

-186-

Lead us not into temptation. Just tell us where it is; we'll find it.

-187-

To strengthen what is right in a fool is a holy task.

∲

-188-

As a rule, the freedom of any people can be judged by the volume of their laughter.

∲

-189-

Nothing in the world is friendlier than a wet dog.

∲

-190-

A relationship without humor is like shaking hands with gloves on.

-191-

Freedom is doing what you like; happiness is liking what you do.

❡

FUNNY BONES

"The average man is more interested in a woman who is interested in him than he is in a woman with beautiful legs."

—Marlene Dietrich

❡

-192-

Very few things in this world so instantly form a common bond among people as laughter. It's a universal language that requires no interpretation.

❡

-193-

One who wishes to cultivate his sense of humor must learn that there are times, at least, when he must free himself from dignity, restraint, and prejudice, and be ready for the great pretences of play.

-194-

In prehistoric times, mankind often had only two choices in crisis situations: fight or flee. In modern times, humor offers us a third alternative: fight, flee—or laugh.

-195-

The most discouraging thing about repeating a good story is that it reminds some idiots of a better one.

∮

-196-

Thomas Alva Edison filled hundreds of notebooks with the results of his experiments—but a few of his notebooks were filled with jokes. He used them to maintain morale and as a shot of comic adrenalin for his overworked staff.

∮

-197-

You can tell when you're on the right track—it's usually uphill.

∮

-198-

Years from now you'll laugh about this; why not start right now?

-199-

The richest laugh is at no one's expense.

∮

-200-

Modern science is still trying to produce a tranquilizer more effective than a few kind words.

∮

-201-

Laughter is the jest medicine.

∮

-202-

We recognize another person's laugh as we would recognize the way they speak.

-203-

Happiness is discovering that the slip of paper under your windshield wiper is just an advertisement.

-204-

Humor is like a needle and thread—deftly used it can patch up just about everything.

∮

-205-

Much of a child's sense of humor, and some of its most boisterous laughter, is created when a child tries to make sense of one of the most complex issues in its life: ADULTS.

∮

-206-

Love may make the world go round, but it's laughter that keeps us from getting dizzy.

∮

-207-

There is nothing wrong with having nothing to say—unless you insist on saying it.

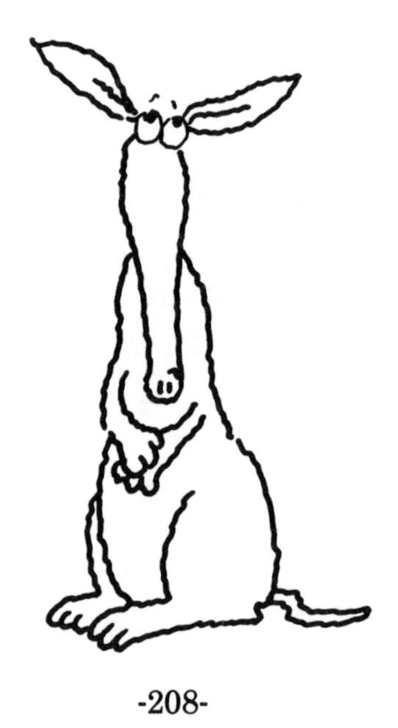

-208-

Forgive, O Lord, my little jokes on Thee
and I'll forgive Thy great big one on me.

-209-

Unlike freedom of the press, laughter is not specifically protected by an amendment to our Constitution. Nevertheless, it is probably the clearest and most resounding expression of freedom we have.

∮

-210-

In this life we all have trouble,
But, when you worry you make them double.
Don't worry, be happy!

∮

FUNNY BONES

The only people who make love all the time are liars.

—Louis Jordan

∮

-211-

You cannot feel depressed if you are laughing. You cannot get an ulcer while you are laughing. Laughter, even forced, can produce endorphins, and you become cheerful.

-212-

After God created the world, he created man and woman. And then to keep the whole thing from collapsing, he created humor.

-213-

Is the outlook BLACK?
Got the BLUES?
GREEN with envy?
Seeing RED?
Color your life with laughter
And soon you will be in the PINK!

∮

-214-

Don't smoke. Don't drink. Go to bed early. Eat plain foods. You may not live any longer, but it will seem like it.

∮

-215-

Perhaps our impulse to enjoy mirth opposes vulnerability to cancer.

∮

-216-

Life is too serious to be taken seriously.

-217-

We worry about our fears and embarassments until we hear some fellow-sufferer who has learned to laugh at the very symptoms that agitate us, and we laugh along feeling we are in company.

-218-

Progress is nothing but the victory of
laughter over dogma.

∮

-219-

Laugh and the world laughs with you.
Snore and you sleep alone.

∮

-220-

The merry laugher is never a hermit, either
in spirit or way of life.

∮

-221-

How to be happy: Keep your heart free
from hate, your mind from worry, live
simply, expect little, give much, sing often,
pray always, forget self, think of others and
their feelings, fill your heart with love,
scatter sunshine. These are tried links in
the golden chain of contentment.

-222-

I tried to tell a few jokes in the sermons. The jokes became so good that I started to charge a cover and a minimum.

-223-

Each of us has a ridiculous side and the child in us is one of our most prized possessions.

∳

-224-

Humor is the healthy way of feeling "distance" between one's self and the problem, a way of standing off and looking at one's problems with perspective.

∳

FUNNY BONES

I only like two kinds of men: domestic and imported.

—Mae West

∳

-225-

You can stay young indefinitely if you eat wisely, get plenty of sleep, work hard, have a positive mental outlook—and lie about your age.

-226-

If you wear a (red) rubber nose for a week
your life will be changed.

-227-

Modesty is the art of drawing attention to whatever it is you are being humble about.

∮

-228-

You can't be truly sexy if you take yourself too seriously or are afraid to make a fool of yourself.

∮

-229-

Managing to have a sense of humor makes it a lot easier to manage people.

∮

-230-

There are two kinds of people at parties—those who want to go home early and those who want to be the last ones in the place. The trouble is that they're usually married to each other.

-231-

Mirth diffuses fear and rage, emotions linked to heart attacks.

∮

-232-

A good laugh is like manure to a farmer—it doesn't do any good until you spread it around.

∮

-233-

Real humor enables you to laugh when someone takes your best joke and improves on it.

∮

-234-

To be playful and serious at the same time is possible, and it defines the ideal mental condition.

-235-

Good humor is a philosophical state of mind. It seems to say to Nature that we take her no more seriously than she takes us.

𝄞

-236-

Humor used to reduce somebody is a slap; humor used to "make it better" is a caress.

𝄞

FUNNY BONES

Rule of Success: Trust only those who stand to lose as much as you when things go wrong.

—Unknown

𝄞

-237-

When I listen to the music of life, I am able to join in the dancing.

-238-

He who laughs last probably intended to tell the story himself.

-239-

The most important asset in business is a sense of humor, and the ability to laugh at yourself or the situation.

§

-240-

In each of us there is a reservoir of joyous freedom.

§

-241-

One of the great gifts you can offer another person is a tidy straight line.

§

-242-

It is more important to have fun than it is to be funny.

-243-

Happiness is learning that your daughter's boyfriend has had his electric guitar repossessed by the finance company.

-244-

The happiness of life is made up of minute fractions—the little, soon-forgotten charities of a kiss or smile, a kind look or heartfelt compliment.

∮

-245-

The main obligation is to amuse yourself.

∮

-246-

Humor is something that causes a tickling of the brain. Laughter is invented to scratch it.

∮

-247-

In general, a spirited environment is marked by laughter—enthusiasm for being on a team and trying darn near anything to make the service or product better.

-248-

The man of understanding finds everything laughable, the man of reason, almost nothing.

∮

-249-

Older people need not undergo a prescribed disengagement from life. Love, friendship, a feeling of connectedness with others, and a sense of humor remain critical to our sense of well-being. As time goes by, we should not forget the redemptive power of smiling, laughing, and hugging.

∮

-250-

S/He who laughs, lasts.

∮

-251-

Cheerfulness is the atmosphere in which all things thrive.

FUNNY BONES

A man usually falls in love with a woman who asks the kinds of questions he is able to answer.

—Ronald Colman

∮

-252-

Humor is the great thing, the saving thing, after all. The minute it crops up, all our hardnesses yield, all our irritations and resentments slip away, and a sunny spirit takes their place.

∮

-253-

There are three rules for creating humor, but unfortunately no one knows what they are.

∮

-254-

A sense of humor can help you overlook the unattractive, tolerate the unpleasant, cope with the unexpected, and smile through the unbearable.

-255-

A good laugh is the best pesticide.

-256-

If you find something to laugh at,
relaxation just happens.

∮

-257-

Life is God's joke on us. It's our mission to
figure out the punchline.

∮

-258-

He deserves Paradise who makes his
companions laugh.

∮

-259-

Anyone who makes us laugh and convinces
us not to take ourselves too seriously is
contributing directly to our physical and
mental well-being. As the most recent
medical research tells us, laughter can be
the best medicine.

-260-

When people become inhuman, or extreme, the first thing they lose is a sense of humor.

-261-

Set me a task in which I can put something of my very self; it is joy; it is art.

∮

-262-

Though we make fun of ourselves for being stupid or lazy or klutzy, by laughing at those flaws, what we are really saying is we're lovable nonetheless.

∮

-263-

Ours is a land of kidding.

∮

-264-

Humor shows you that the foibles and the weakness that you encounter every day are shared by everyone.

-265-

The art of medicine consists of amusing the patient while nature cures the disease.

-266-

Man is born with a capacity for laughter and merriment.

∮

-267-

Pleasant sights and good reports give happiness and health.

∮

-268-

Humor is an affirmation of dignity, a declaration on man's superiority to all that befalls him.

∮

FUNNY BONES

Men have a much better time of it than women; for one thing, they marry later; for another thing, they die earlier.

—H. L. Mencken

-269-

Professions, like nations, are civilized to the extent they can satirize themselves.

∮

-270-

Wit is the sudden marriage of ideas which before their marriage were not perceived to have any relationship.

∮

-271-

Question: Why can angels fly?
Answer: Because, they take themselves lightly.

∮

-272-

I think the next best thing to solving a problem is finding some humor in it.

-273-

Laugh at yourself first, before anyone else can.

-274-

The place to be happy is here, the time to be happy is now, the way to be happy is to make others so.

∮

-275-

Where humor is concerned, there are no standards—no one can say what is good or bad, although you can be sure that everyone will.

∮

-276-

Humor and laughter should be part of any strategy for coping with disease or illness.

∮

-277-

The gods are fond of a joke.

-278-

Joking about death—or anything else that oppresses us—makes it less frightening.

-279-

True humor springs not more from the head than the heart; it is not contempt, its essence is love; it issues not in laughter, but in still smiles which lie far deeper.

∳

-280-

Laughter loves company even more than misery loves company.

∳

-281-

Why humor? Why not humor? I'd rather it be my ally than my enemy.

∳

-282-

God's favorite music is said to be laughter.

-283-

Humor provides us with a valuable tool for maintaining an inner strength in the midst of outer turmoil.

∮

-284-

Humor is your own smile surprising you in the mirror.

∮

-285-

There's no record of anyone who ever died from laughing.

∮

FUNNY BONES

By all means marry: If you get a good wife, you'll become happy; if you get a bad one, you'll become a philosopher.

—Socrates

-286-

Shortly after Adam had been created, he complained, "O, Lord! You have given the lion fierce teeth and claws, and the elephant formidable tusks; you have given the deer swiftness of legs, and the turtle a protective shell; you have given the birds flight of wings, but you have left me altogether defenseless." And the Lord said unto Adam, "I shall give you an invisible weapon that will serve you and your children better than any weapons of fight or flight, a power that will save you even from yourself. I shall give you the sense of humor."

-287-

Laughter is the tonic relief, surcease for pain.

-288-

The man who gets along in the world is the one who can look cheerful and happy when he isn't.

∮

-289-

It wouldn't surprise me if there was a measurable correlation between humor in an administration and the popularity of that administration's policies.

∮

-290-

He who hesitates is not only lost but several miles from the next exit.

∮

-291-

What greater joy than to arise with the dawn of each new day when the whole world beckons us to meet its never-ending mysteries. What greater joy than to seize all life has to offer and to make the most of what we have and who we are as we prepare the way to a bright and beautiful tomorrow.

-292-

Some wives are so concerned about their husband's happiness that they hire a private detective to find out the cause of it.

-293-

A merry heart doeth good like a medicine.

∮

FUNNY BONES

There may be some things better than sex, and there may be some things worse. But there's nothing exactly like it.

—W. C. Fields

∮

-294-

The glow of one warm thought is to me worth more than money.

∮

-295-

Prepare for mirth, for mirth becomes a feast.

-296-

Humor is laughing at what you haven't got
when you ought to have it.

∮

-297-

Warning: Humor may be hazardous to
your illness.

∮

-298-

You're never fully dressed without a smile.

∮

-299-

A jest's prosperity lies more in the ear of
the listener than in the mouth of
the speaker.

-300-

When we provide an environment that is pleasant and multidimensional⅔fun!-we inspire people. They look at things differently. They become more creative and productive.

∮

-301-

A comedian is just like any other average American who stays up all night and sleeps ‘til noon.

∮

-302-

The funniest character I ever drew was in my bathroom mirror.

∮

-303-

Science has not yet found a cure for the pun.

-304-

It's never too late to have a happy childhood.

-305-

Old jokes never die. They just smell that way.

∮

-306-

Humor is an end within itself. It satisfies.

∮

-307-

The smile on your face is a light to tell people that your heart is home.

∮

-308-

Through humor one can raise issues that you would not otherwise bring up.

-309-

Laughter costs too much when it is purchased by sacrificing dignity.

-310-

A man hath no better thing under the sun
than to eat and to drink and to be merry.

∮

-311-

Avoid cliches like the plague.

∮

-312-

I won't grow up.
I don't wanna wear a tie
And a serious expression
In the middle of July!

∮

-313-

Wit is educated insolence.

-314-

A wise teacher makes learning a joy.

∮

-315-

I don't know what humor is. Anything
that's funny—tragedy or anything, it don't
make no difference so long as you happen
to hit it just right. But there's one thing
I'm proud of—I ain't got it in for anybody.
I don't like to make jokes that hurt anybody.

∮

-316-

If you don't think people have good
memories, try repeating a joke you told
them about a month ago.

∮

-317-

Humor is an enjoyable juggling with social taboos.

-318-

God grant me the serenity to accept the things I cannot change, the courage to change the things I can, and the wisdom to know the difference . . . and a sense of humor when I don't know the difference.

-319-

Laughter is God's remedy for fear.

∮

FUNNY BONES

Choose a job you love, and you will never have to work a day in your life.

—Confucius

∮

-320-

There is truth in humor as much as there is humor in truth.

∮

-321-

Humor reaches out and puts its arm around the listener and says, "I am one of you, I understand."

-322-

The fully integrated person is capable of a harmonious blending of the "adult" and the "child."

In matters of humor, what is appealing to one person may be appalling to another.

∳

-324-

If you cannot laugh at yourself, you will find plenty of volunteers to do it for you.

∳

-325-

Geniune happiness is when a wife sees a double chin on her husband's old girlfriend.

∳

-326-

Humor sells. Humor convinces. Humor instructs. Humor entertains. Humor communicates . . . Humor is the ideal vehicle to capture interest, attention, and approval.

-327-

To get 'em listening, get 'em laughing.

∮

-328-

The best doctors in the world are Dr. Quiet,
Dr. Diet, and Dr. Merryman.

∮

-329-

Take your responsibilities seriously, but
take yourself lightly.

∮

-330-

Instead of working for the survival of the
fittest, we should be working for the
survival of the wittiest, then we can all
die laughing.

-331-

The sun does not shine for a few trees and flowers, but for the wide world's joy.

-332-

Joke telling can be a lot of fun. Or it can be a disaster, like the man who told a joke and everyone booed except one man: he was applauding the booing.

∮

-333-

A laugh is worth a hundred groans in any market.

∮

-334-

There is no cure for birth or death save to enjoy the interval.

∮

-335-

My way of joking is to tell the truth; it's the funniest joke in the world.

-336-

Humor is a proof of faith.

∮

-337-

Crack up with laughter before you crack up with stress.

∮

-338-

Frame your mind to mirth and merriment, which bar a thousand harms and lengthen life.

∮

-339-

Very few things in this world so instantly form a common bond among people as laughter. It's a universal language that requires no interpretation.

-340-

People will pay more to be entertained than educated.

-341-

Even the gods love jokes.

∮

-342-

There are two ways to be clever. First, think of a bright remark in time to say it. Second, think of it in time not to say it.

∮

-343-

We have a lot of evidence that shows mirth and laughter affect most of the major physical systems of the body. You can get a really good workout from it . . . It's not as vigorous as calisthentics or training in terms of intensity, but you can laugh a lot more times a day than you can do push-ups.

∮

-344-

Were it not for my little jokes, I could not bear the burden of this office.

-345-

We are most unfair to God if we do not allow him to laugh.

-346-

Laughter is like changing a baby's diaper—it doesn't permanently solve any problems, but it makes things more acceptable for a while.

∮

-347-

A happy face means a glad heart; a sad face means a breaking heart.

∮

-348-

Keep your face to the sunshine and you cannot see the shadows.

∮

-349-

A beautiful day is like a good friend,
Bringing so many moments of joy.

-350-

Happy laughter and family voices in the home will keep more kids off the streets at night than the strictest curfew.

∮

-351-

The good joke is ageless. Even the oldest joke is always new to some, and, cleverly embellished and properly modernized, the chestnut often becomes the latest gag of the comedians of stage, radio, and television.

∮

-352-

Science opens to us the book of nature; comedy, the book of human nature.

∮

-353-

What soap is to the body, laughter is to the soul.

-354-

When humor goes, there goes civilization.

-355-

What is comedy? Comedy is the art of making people laugh without making them puke.

∮

-356-

My method is to take the utmost trouble to find the right thing to say, and then to say it with the utmost levity.

∮

-357-

All children benefit from a combination of work and play.

∮

-358-

Laughter lifts us over high ridges and lights up dark valleys in a way that makes life so much easier.

-359-

You must play the fool a little if you would not be thought wholly a fool.

∮

-360-

Humor is just another defense against the universe.

∮

-361-

Nonsense makes the heart grow fonder.

∮

-362-

Man is only fully human when he is at play.

∮

-363-

Only a brilliant fool can write comedy.

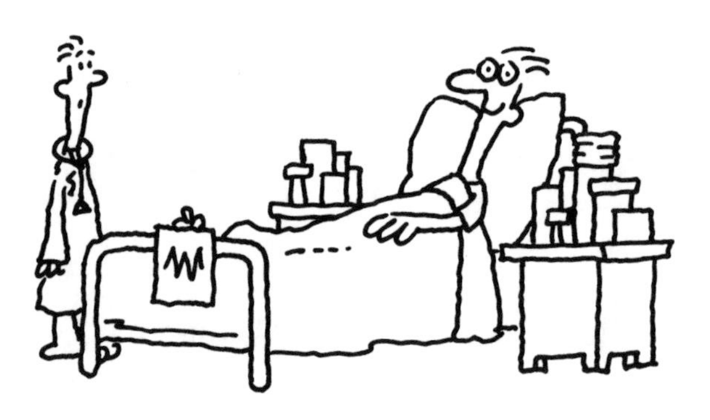

-364-

Get-well cards have become so humorous that if you don't get sick you're missing half the fun.

-365-

Like a welcome summer rain, humor may suddenly cleanse and cool the earth, the air and you.

∮

-366-

Fear not a jest. If one throws salt at thee thou wilt receive no harm unless there are sore places.

∮

-367-

Stop acting as if you have the rest of your life.

∮

-368-

Genuine humor is always kindly and gracious. It points out the weakness of humanity, but shows no contempt and leaves no sting.

-369-

He deserves Paradise who makes his companion laugh.

∮

-370-

If the world laughs at you, laugh right back—it's as funny as you are.

∮

-371-

Do a few good turns today. You won't get dizzy.

∮

-372-

Man is the only animal that laughs and weeps; for he is the only animal that is struck with the difference between what things are, and what they ought to be.

-373-

The human race has only one really
effective weapon and that is laughter.

-374-

For all the austerities and rigors of Zen, and the serenity of its religious vision, in it the Chinese dragon smiles and the Indian Buddha roars with laughter.

∮

-375-

What you don't know may not hurt you, but it will certainly amuse a lot of people.

∮

FUNNY BONES

A business is too big when it takes a week for gossip to go from one end of the office to the other.

—Unknown

∮

-376-

The real wit tells jokes to make others feel superior, while the half-wit tells them to make others feel small.

-377-

Laughter: an audible smile.

∮

-378-

Wit is a sword; it is meant to make people feel the point as well as see it.

∮

-379-

I can't be happy every day but, at least, I can be cheerful.

∮

FUNNY BONES

Among the chief worries of today's business executives is the large number of unemployed still on the payrolls.

-380-

If you drink, don't drive. Don't even putt.

-381-

A fun working environment is more productive than a routine environment. People who enjoy their work will come up with more ideas. The fun is contagious and everybody works harder to get a piece of that fun.

∮

-382-

Gaff and the world laughs with you.

∮

-383-

It seems to me that deep relating without joy, laughter, and a sense of humor is an impossibility.

∮

-384-

Laughter is God's hand on the shoulder of a troubled world.

FUNNY BONES

Many a man has fallen in love with a girl in a light so dim he would not have chosen a suit by it.

—Maurice Chevalier

∮

-385-

Losing your sense of humor is no laughing matter.

∮

-386-

In the sweetness of friendship let there be laughter, and sharing of pleasures.

∮

-387-

Better a witty fool than a foolish wit.

-388-

One doesn't have a sense of humor. It has you.

-389-

Joy sings in beauty that surrounds us . . .
Joy smiles through loved ones all around us . . .
Joy speaks in gentle words that guide us . . .
Joy glows in feelings deep inside us . . .

∮

-390-

Notice happy things! Keep a notebook
of things you have to be
happy/thankful about.

∮

-391-

Affirm happy things! Tell yourself your life
is happy and, eventually, it will be.

∮

-392-

People like to hear a story that represents a
lesson or point of learning. It's a tradition
that has gone on since before Old
Testament days.

-393-

Grinners are winners.

-394-

Humor: Everyone's everyday magic.

∳

-395-

Teach happy things! You can have a positive influence wherever you go if the message you communicate is that life is beautiful. Make sure the people closest to you know how wonderful they are.

∳

-396-

The pursuit of happiness seems to be the chase of a lifetime.

∳

-397-

Think young. Aging is for wine.

-398-

Comedy is supposed to make you feel good about yourself and good about your neighbor and to laugh about something that's troubling you. Comedy is relief.

∮

-399-

He who laughs most, learns best.

∮

-400-

Humor may be defined as the kindly contemplation of the incongruities of life and the artistic expression thereof.

∮

-401-

Anything that develops general intelligence, such as reading, travel, social contacts, should tend to develop also one's sense of humor.

-402-

Nothing is quite as funny as the unintended humor of reality.

-403-

The skills of exaggeration, reversal, association, spontaneity, juxtaposition and paradox are all involved in creativity and humor.

∮

-404-

All the days of the afflicted are bad, but a cheerful heart has a continual feast.

∮

-405-

Hope is a light diet, but very stimulating.

∮

-406-

Security is a smile from a headwaiter.

-407-

There are three laughing sages of Hu-hsi, overcome with mirth in every painting, as if a Zen trinity were enjoying some eternal joke.

∮

-408-

Humor is immediately obvious as one of the outstanding folkways of all Americans.

∮

-409-

Wit is the salt of conversation, not the food.

∮

FUNNY BONES

The honeymoon is over when he phones to say he'll be late for supper and she's already left a note that it's in the refrigerator.

-410-

If the soup had been as warm as the wine, and the wine as old as the fish, and the fish as young as the maid, and the maid as willing as the hostess, it would have been a very good meal.

∲

-411-

Smiles reach the hard-to-reach places.

∲

-412-

I will remember that my laughter and song are also ways of praying.

∲

-413-

No family should attempt an auto trip if their kids outnumber the car windows.

-414-

Dying is easy. Comedy is difficult.

If you want to be well-liked never lie about yourself—and be careful about telling the truth about others.

∮

-416-

A witty, devastating answer in an argument is like swatting a fly: by the time you've thought of it, the opportunity has flown.

∮

-417-

A smile never goes up in price or down in value.

∮

FUNNY BONES

Don't assume that every sad-eyed woman has loved and lost—she may have got him.

-418-

They that are serious in ridiculous things will be ridiculous in serious things.

∮

-419-

A person without a sense of humor is like a wagon without springs —jolted by every pebble in the road.

∮

-420-

Ten minutes of genuine belly laughter had an anesthetic effect and would give me at least two hours of pain-free sleep.

∮

FUNNY BONES

When they say a man is a "born executive" they mean his father owns the business.

-421-

Anything worth taking seriously is worth making fun of.

-422-

There's no time like the pleasant.

∮

-423-

Good-hearted ethnic humor in America has largely vanished. Too bad for America.

∮

Laughter oft is but an art
To drown the outcry of the heart.

∮

-425-

The Zen tradition, according to legend, begins with a smile. . . . This smile is the signature of the sudden realization of the "point," and the joyful approval of its significance. It is the smile of Truth, or Truth smiling.

-426-

People who laugh at death feel superior to those who are dead.

∮

-427-

God preserve us from those who have no sense of humor, for they are the scourge of humankind.

∮

-428-

Humor communicates more effectively than almost any narrative or recitation of details. People forget concepts, facts and figures, but they remember a joke.

∮

-429-

Humor is the hole that lets sawdust out of a stuffed shirt.

-430-

You are only young once, but you can remain immature indefinitely.

-431-

There are now 175 million people, census takers tell us, in this blessed land of ours, and as I write this probably fifty million of them are telling a story.

∮

-432-

. . . The person who can bring the spirit of laughter into a room is indeed blessed.

∮

-433-

By its nature humor is anarchistic and implies, when it does not state, criticism of existing institutions, beliefs, and functionaries.

∮

-434-

As literature, humor is so compelling and pleasurable and infectious that it will win over to enjoyable reading many students with whom other approaches have proved hopeless.

-435-

Write on your hearts that every day is the best day of the year.

∮

-436-

The world will end in joy, because it is a place of sorrow.
When joy has come, the purpose of the world has gone.
The world will end in peace, because it is a place of war.
When peace has come, what is the purpose of the world?
The world will end in laughter, because it is a place of tears.
Where there is laughter, who can longer weep?
And only complete forgiveness brings all this to bless the world.
In blessing it departs, for it will not end as it began.

∮

-437-

Wit comes from the intellect, humor comes from emotion, and fun comes from imagination.

-438-

Those who do not know how to weep do not know how to laugh either.

∮

FUNNY BONES

Doing business without advertising is like winking at a person in the dark. You know what you're doing, but nobody else does.

—Stewart Britt

∮

-439-

I found out soon
That to be a buffoon
Is a serious thing as a rule.
For a jester's chief employment
Is to kill himself
For your enjoyment,
And a jester unemployed
Is nobody's fool.

—Sylvia Fine

". . .etc.,"

(more coming!)

A Few Thoughts On Enjoying Life Now

"It is not your lot to weep, and you were not put here to suffer. To find value in suffering is to condemn yourself to hell. The spirit that created you would not have its children in pain. Wake up, arise, and go on your way with laughter in your heart! Wipe away your tears and live in love! You may explore every highway, byway, mountain, and valley of this world, and no matter how far you travel or how many years you search, you will come to this very conclusion: Life is for loving, joy, and celebration—now!"

—Alan Cohen

"We are substantially different people capable of substantially different things at the various stages of our lives. Our attitudes, philosophies, talents, and enthusiasms go through surprising transformations—and once gone, can rarely be revisited . . . At every stage of your creative life, drain the cup dry . . . These are unique moments in your life for turning out pages or performances that you may not feel motivated to produce, or able to produce, five or ten years from now."

—Robert Orben

"The trip you can enjoy today because of the person you are, may be a frustratingly unhappy one tomorrow because of the person you have become in the meantime. Go, wherever you have always wanted to go. Go as soon as you can, for as far as you can, for as long as you can."

—Bob and Patti Carpenter

"Accept the fact that life is like fording a river, stepping from one slippery stone to another, and you must rejoice every time you don't lose your balance, and learn to laugh at all the times you do."

—Merle Shain

"If you pile up enough tomorrows, you'll find you've collected nothing but a lot of empty yesterdays."

—Professor Harold Hill, The Music Man

If I Had My Life To Live Over

I'd like to make more mistakes next time. I'd relax. I would limber up. I would be sillier than I have been this trip. I would take fewer things seriously. I would take more chances. I would climb more mountains and swim more rivers. I would eat more ice cream and less beans.
I would perhaps have more actual troubles, but I'd have fewer imaginary ones.

You see, I'm one of those people who live sensibly
and sanely hour after hour, day after day. Oh, I've had my moments, and if I had it to do over again, I'd have more of them. In fact, I'd try to have nothing else. Just moments, one after another, instead of living so many years ahead of each day. I've been one of those persons who never goes anywhere without a thermometer, a hot water bottle, a raincoat, and a parachute. If I had to do it again, I would travel lighter than I have.

If I had my life to live over, I would start barefoot earlier in the spring and stay that way later in the fall. I would go to more dances. I would ride more merry-go-rounds. I would pick more daisies.

Nadine Stair,
85 years old,
Louisville, Kentucky

Slow Me Down, Lord! *

Slow me down, Lord!
Ease the pounding of my heart by the quieting of my mind.
Steady my hurried pace with a vision of the eternal reach of time.

Give me, amid the confusion of the day, the calmness of the everlasting hills.
Break the tensions of my nerves and muscles
with the soothing music of the singing streams that
still live in my memory. Help me to know the magical,
restoring power of sleep.

Teach me the art of taking minute vacations -
of slowing down to look at a flower, to chat with a friend,
to pat a dog, to answer a child's question, to read a few lines
from a good book.

Remind me each day of the fable of the hare and the
tortoise, that I may know that the race is not always to the
swift - that there is more to life than increasing its speed.
Let me look upward into the branches of the towering oak
and know that it grew slowly and well.

*Excerpted with permission from INSIGHT, the monthly audiocassette program by Earl Nightingale. Copyright ©1987 by Nightingale-Conant Corporation, 7300 N. Lehigh Ave., Chicago, IL 60648.

How can I improve my service to those
people I've selected to serve?
What can I do to make their lives better
somehow
because I was born and because I
understand the system now?
I know that my rewards all the years of my
life will be
in exact proportion to my service. As I sow,
so shall I reap,
all the years of my life. My job is to find
ways to improve my sowing -
to sow a better, richer crop, a more
nutritious crop.
And as I sow abundantly, so will I reap the
abundant harvest.

Let me step out of line and start to think
for myself with my own astonishing brain.
Let me bring to bear upon the lives of those
I serve my own unique and personal
contribution to add to the total. I know
there are ways of doing
everything on earth better than it's being
done now. Let me see some of those
ways.

I need not worry myself about my harvest.
I need concern myself only with the
sowing. I need only improve my input, and
the rewards will take care of
themselves.

Slow me down, Lord, and inspire me to
send my roots
deep into the soil of life's enduring values,
that I may grow more surely toward the
stars.

And make me remember why I'm here,
Lord. I'm here to
serve other people. Every day of my life,
I'm served by
thousands of human beings I never even
see. They operate
my utilities, and they built my home and
supply my food
and every single thing I use during every
24-hour period
of my lifetime. They made my bedding, my
clothes, my
appliances, my car - my God, it's endless.
And I can't even thank them,
except through my service in turn.

You Are Entitled To Joy

Humor, laughter, playfulness, and joy are so important to you. They are your natural intended state. They are both the tools for being more peaceful and fulfilled and the results of finding peace and fulfillment.

If you are like most other souls, bound to the pressures and urgencies of apparently "serious" matters on a daily basis, you need to lighten up. In this part of life's journey we find many distortions of perceptions which stress us and wear us down and make us sick.

A relaxed attitude which comes from feeling safe, secure, and unhurried is fostered by and the result of a playful attitude. Merely "being" would be enough to maintain a state of joy and yet so many of us find ourselves too busy to just be.

Joy can be found in a myriad of actions and interests. You can make joy a practice in your life. You can find your personal way to truth and happiness, health, fulfillment, brightness, cheer, love and peace.

If you are still wondering what there is to be joyful about, consider this list of titles gleaned from the card catalogue at my local library. Each of these represents the written expression of joyful sharing by a person who has made a discovery of happiness. Perhaps one of these is yours, too.

The Joy of Aging
The Joy of a Small Garden
The Joy of Backyard Boat Building
The Joy of Beauty
The Joy of Being Human
The Joy of Being Single
The Joy of Being Sober
The Joy of Birding
Joyous Birthing
The Joy of CB
The Joyful Child
The Joy of Christmas
Joy in the Classroom
The Joy of Cocktails and Hors d'Oeuvre
The Joy of Computer Communication
The Joy of Cooking
The Joy of Cookies
The Joy of Feeling: Bodymind Acupressure
The Joy of Gardening
The Joy of Flying Paper Airplanes
The Joy of Gardening Cookbook
The Joy of Gay Sex
The Joy of Geraniums
The Joy of Giving Homemade Food
The Joy of Grilling
The Joy of Hand Weaving
The Joy of Ice Cream
The Joy of International Cooking
The Joy of Jumping Rope
The Joy of Living The Joy of Living
Salt-free
The Joy of Man's Desiring
The Joy of Mathematics

The Joy of Minis and Micros (computers)
The Joy of Music
The Joy of Nature
The Joy of Oil Painting
The Joy of Owning a Shih Tzu
The Joy of Pasta
The Joy of Photography
The Joy of Quilting
The Joy of Reading
The Joy of Running
The Joy of Seafood
The Joy of Sensual Massage
The Joy of Sex
The Joy of Snorkeling
The Joy of Snow
The Joy of Soaring
The Joy of Spinning
The Joy of Stress
The Joy of Stuffed Preppies
The Joy of The Only Child
The Joy of Twins
The Joy of Words
The Joy of Working

Face it. If someone can find joy in *Mathematics* or *Stress*, surely you can find something to celebrate! How about The Joy of *YOU*? Well, check out these books, or read the funnies, or go to a comedy club, or look at cloud shapes, or . . . whatever turns you on. That is, of course, right after eating dessert first!

Index by Quotation Number

62 Hunter Adams, M.D.
63 Leo Burnett
64 Lynn Cassan
65 Orion Swett Marden
66 Harold Bloomfield, M.D.
67 Hunter Adams, M.D.
68 Unknown
69 Alan Cohen
70 Lorraine Risly
71 Harold Bloomfield, M.D.
72 Jim Boren
73 Henri De Mondeville
74 Unknown
75 Myron Cohen
76 Alan Cohen
77 Unknown
78 Unknown
79 Josh Billings
80 Janet Woititz
81 Unknown
82 Alan Cohen
83 Unknown
84 Unknown
85 Jean Westcott
86 Unknown
87 Unknown
88 William Blake
89 Lorraine Kisly
90 Charles Chaplin
91 Janet Woititz
92 Allen Klein
93 Bob Basso
94 Egon Friedell
95 Unknown
96 Unknown
97 Leo Buscaglia
98 Unknown
99 Ogden Nash
100 E. B. White
101 Elbert Hubbard
102 Steve Wilson
103 Susan Smith Jones
104 Bernie Siegal, M.D.
105 George Bernard Shaw
106 Unknown
107 Unknown
108 Susan Smith Jones
109 Lucille Ball
110 Steve Wilson
111 Alan Cohen
112 Unknown
113 Unknown
114 W. Brugh Joy, M.D.
115 Psychology Today
116 Song Title
117 Maxwell Maltz
118 Larry Klein
119 Will Rogers
120 Harvey Mindess, Ph.d.
121 Dale Irvin
122 Mark Twain
123 Maxwell Maltz
124 Father Tom Walsh
125 James Free
126 Jack Wilson
127 Steve Wilson
128 Sharon Yoder
129 Unknown
130 Susan Smith Jones
131 Albert Einstein

132 Unknown
133 Charles Chaplin
134 Steve Wilson
135 Joseph Bruchac
136 Victor Borge
137 Peter Marsh
138 Joseph Bruchac
139 Ramtha
140 Unknown
141 Unknown
142 Unknown
143 John Cleese
144 Owen Meredith
145 Arthur Parker
146 Vera Robinson
147 Teilhard de Chardin
148 Tom Nansbury
149 Unknown
150 Joseph Bruchac
151 Alvin Schwartz
152 Ken Blanchard
153 Will Rogers
154 Unknown
155 Unknown
156 Richard Lewis
157 Unknown
158 James Thurber
159 Steve Wilson
160 Ken Blanchard
161 Touchstones
162 Roger Von Oech
163 Robert Orben
164 William Novak
165 Robert Louis Stevenson
166 Katherine Ferrari
167 Herbert Prochnow
168 Unknown
169 Steve Wilson
170 Unknown
171 Leo Buscaglia
172 Isaac Asimov
173 Joey Adams
174 Unknown
175 Mencius
176 Maxwell Maltz
177 Alexander Pope
178 Shirley Wilson
179 Maxwell Maltz
180 Unknown
181 Fred Pryor
182 Unknown
183 Unknown
184 Maxwell Maltz
185 Fred Pryor
186 Sam Levenson
187 I Ching
188 Unknown
189 Dan Bennett
190 Sherry Suib Cohen
191 Unknown
192 Leo Buscaglia
193 Max J. Herzberg
194 Robert Orben
195 Unknown
196 Robert Orben
197 Unknown
198 Steve Wilson
199 Linda Loving

200 Unknown
201 Joel Goodman
202 Richard Lewis
203 Unknown
204 Unknown
205 Richard Lewis
206 Donald Zochert
207 Unknown
208 Robert Frost
209 Gerald R. Ford
210 Bobby McFerrin
211 Lendon Smith, M.D.
212 Ernie Hoberecht
213 Steve Wilson
214 Unknown
215 William Fry, Jr., M.D.
216 Oscar Wilde
217 Max J. Herzberg
218 Benjamin DeCasseres
219 Anthony Burgess
220 Max J. Herzberg
221 Unknown
222 Jackie Mason
223 Leo Buscaglia
224 Rollo May
225 Unknown
226 Hunter Adams, M.D.
227 Unknown
228 Unknown
229 Steve Wilson
230 Unknown
231 William Fry, Jr., M.D.
232 Michael Prichard
233 Unknown
234 John Dewey
235 M. Dale Baughman
236 Lotus Weinstock
237 Katherine Long
238 Unknown
239 Mark H. McCormack
240 Leo Buscaglia
241 Paul Dickson
242 Lawrence J. Peter
243 Unknown
244 Samuel Taylor Coleridge
245 S. J. Perelman
246 Unknown
247 Tom Peters
248 Goethe
249 Alvin F. Poussaint, M.D.
250 Walter Lippman
251 Jean Paul Richter
252 Mark Twain
253 Laurence Peter
254 Moshe Waldoks
255 Vladimir Nabakov
256 Kay Ann Herth, R.N.
257 John Guarrine
258 Mohammed
259 Leo Buscaglia
260 Moshe Waldoks
261 Bliss Carman
262 Harvey Mindess, Ph.D.
263 L. H. Robbins
264 Moshe Waldoks
265 Voltaire
266 Max J. Herzberg
267 Proverbs

268 Romain Gary
269 Peter De Vries
270 Mark Twain
271 Unknown
272 Frank Clark
273 Elsa Maxwell
274 Unknown
275 John Kenneth Galbraith
276 Norman Cousins
277 Aristotle
278 Allen Klein
279 Thomas Carlyle
280 Joel Goodman
281 Robert Orben
282 Ralph Blum
283 Brian Deery
284 Langston Hughes
285 Lucille Nahemow
286 Old Legend
287 Charles Chaplin
288 Unknown-Uncertain
289 Gerald R. Ford
290 Unknown
291 Paul Conrad
292 Unknown
293 Proverbs
294 Thomas Jefferson
295 William Shakespeare
296 Langston Hughes
297 Unknown
298 Annie
299 William Shakespeare
300 Fred Pryor
301 Myron Cohen
302 Michael Senett
303 Robert Byrne
304 Unknown
305 Unknown
306 Fred Pryor
307 Allen Klein
308 Moshe Waldoks
309 Unknown
310 Ecclesiastes
311 Unknown
312 Peter Pan
313 Aristotle
314 Proverbs
315 Will Rogers
316 Unknown
317 Max J. Herzberg
318 After Niebuhr Goodman, Joel
319 Alan Cohen
320 Steve Wilson
321 Robert Orben
322 Susan Smith Jones
323 Mel Helitzer
324 Peter G. Hanson, M.D.
325 Unknown
326 Robert Orben
327 Allen Klein
328 Jonathan Swift
329 Unknown
330 Lilly Tomlin
331 Henry Ward Beecher
332 Bob Phillips
333 Charles Lamb
334 George Santayana

335 George Bernard Shaw
336 Charles Shulz
337 Unknown
338 William Shakespeare
339 Leo Buscaglia
340 Johnny Carson
341 Plato
342 Unknown
343 William Fry, Jr., M.D.
344 Abraham Lincoln
345 Frederick W. Nietzche
346 Unknown
347 Proverbs
348 Helen Keller
349 Leslie Ann Howe
350 Max J. Herzberg
351 Lewis Copeland
352 Evan Esar
353 Jewish Proverb
354 Erma Bombeck
355 Steve Martin
356 George Bernard Shaw
357 Jean Marzollo
358 Alan Cohen
359 Michael De Montaigne
360 Mel Brooks
361 Carolyn Wells
362 Schiller
363 James McConnell
364 Earl Wilson
365 Langston Hughes
366 Latin Proverb
367 Steve Wilson
368 Unknown
369 Mohammed
370 Unknown
371 Unknown
372 William Hazlett
373 Mark Twain
374 Conrad Hyer
375 Unknown
376 Elmer Wheeler
377 Unknown
378 G. K. Chesterton
379 Beverly Sills
380 Unknown
381 Roger Von Oech
382 Aaron Abbott
383 Leo Buscaglia
384 Bettenell Huntzicker
385 Steve Wilson
386 Kahlil Gibran
387 Unknown
388 Larry Gelbart
389 Barbara Burrow
390 Susan Jeffers
391 Susan Jeffers
392 David Pfreim
393 Unknown
394 Steve Wilson
395 Susan Jeffers
396 Unknown
397 Unknown
398 Sid Caesar
399 John Cleese
400 Steven Leacock
401 Winifred H. Nash
402 Steve Allen

403 Norman Cousins
404 Proverbs
405 Balzac
406 Russell Baker
407 Conrad Hyers
408 Max J. Herzberg
409 William Hazlett
410 Unknown
411 Steve Wilson
412 Touchstones
413 Teresa Bloomingdale
414 Edmund Gwenn
415 Unknown
416 Unknown
417 Emmanuel
418 Henry Ward Beecher
419 Norman Cousins
420 Cato the Elder
421 Tom Lehrer
422 Oliver Hereford
423 Gene Shalit
424 C. G. Jung
425 Conrad Hyers
426 Fred Allen
427 Leo Rosten
428 Robert Orben
429 Unknown
430 Art Gliner
431 Bennett Cerf
432 Bennett Cerf
433 Malcolm Muggeridge
434 Max J. Herzberg
435 Ralph Waldo Emerson
436 A Course in Miracles
437 Rita Mae Brown
438 Golda Meir
439 Sylvia Fine

Index by Author's Last Name

Do you have a favorite quotation about laughter or play that you would like to see in the next book? Please send it to us and join the fun. (Please send quote and source.)

Send to:

Applied Humor Systems
3400 N. High Street #120
Columbus, OH 43202

To order more copies of 'Eat Dessert First,'
please fill out and mail one of the self-addressed forms below.

Your NAME: ____________________
ADDRESS: ____________________
____
City: __________ State: _____ Zip __________

Send check or money order to:
Applied Humor Systems
3400 N. High Street #120
Columbus, OH 43202

Quantity	Item	Price	Total
	Eat Dessert First	12.95	
	SUBTOTAL		
	Ohio Residents Add 5.75% Tax		
	Shipping and Handling—U.S. $2.95 • Foreign—U.S. $7.45		
	Total Enclosed		

Charge to my MasterCard # ____________ or Visa # ____________
Signature ____________ Expiration Date ____________

MasterCard or Visa: PHONE your Order to 614-268-1094, OR
FAX with card # , expiration date, and signature to 614-263-LAFF (5233)

Your NAME: ____________________
ADDRESS: ____________________
____
City: __________ State: _____ Zip __________

Send check or money order to:
Applied Humor Systems
3400 N. High Street #120
Columbus, OH 43202

Quantity	Item	Price	Total
	Eat Dessert First	12.95	
	SUBTOTAL		
	Ohio Residents Add 5.75% Tax		
	Shipping and Handling—U.S. $2.95 • Foreign—U.S. $7.45		
	Total Enclosed		

Charge to my MasterCard # ____________ or Visa # ____________
Signature ____________ Expiration Date ____________

MasterCard or Visa: PHONE your Order to 614-268-1094, OR
FAX with card # , expiration date, and signature to 614-263-LAFF (5233)

To order more copies of 'Eat Dessert First,'
please fill out and mail one of the self-addressed forms below.

Your NAME: ______________________
ADDRESS: ______________________
____
City: __________ State: _____ Zip __________

Send check or money order to:
Applied Humor Systems
3400 N. High Street #120
Columbus, OH 43202

Quantity	Item	Price	Total
	Eat Dessert First	12.95	
	SUBTOTAL		
	Ohio Residents Add 5.75% Tax		
	Shipping and Handling—U.S. $2.95 • Foreign—U.S. $7.45		
	Total Enclosed		

Charge to my MasterCard # ______________ or Visa # ______________
Signature ______________ Expiration Date ______________

MasterCard or Visa: PHONE your Order to 614-268-1094, OR
FAX with card # , expiration date, and signature to 614-263-LAFF (5233)

Your NAME: ______________________
ADDRESS: ______________________
____
City: __________ State: _____ Zip __________

Send check or money order to:
Applied Humor Systems
3400 N. High Street #120
Columbus, OH 43202

Quantity	Item	Price	Total
	Eat Dessert First	12.95	
	SUBTOTAL		
	Ohio Residents Add 5.75% Tax		
	Shipping and Handling—U.S. $2.95 • Foreign—U.S. $7.45		
	Total Enclosed		

Charge to my MasterCard # ______________ or Visa # ______________
Signature ______________ Expiration Date ______________

MasterCard or Visa: PHONE your Order to 614-268-1094, OR
FAX with card # , expiration date, and signature to 614-263-LAFF (5233)